THE GENDER
WAGE GAP

BY MELISSA HIGGINS AND MICHAEL REGAN

CONTENT CONSULTANT

SHANNON N. DAVIS, PhD
ASSOCIATE PROFESSOR OF SOCIOLOGY
GEORGE MASON UNIVERSITY

Essential Library

An Imprint of Abdo Publishing | abdopublishing.com

abdopublishing.com

Published by Abdo Publishing, a division of ABDO, PO Box 398166, Minneapolis, Minnesota 55439. Copyright © 2017 by Abdo Consulting Group, Inc. International copyrights reserved in all countries. No part of this book may be reproduced in any form without written permission from the publisher. Essential Library™ is a trademark and logo of Abdo Publishing.

Printed in the United States of America, North Mankato, Minnesota
092016
012017

Cover Photo: Mitchell Leff/Getty Images
Interior Photos: Stewart Cook/Rex Features/AP Images, 4–5; Shutterstock Images, 7, 29, 38–39, 63; Rodriguez/TNS/Newscom, 10; North Wind Picture Archives, 14–15; Abbie Rowe/White House Photograph/John F. Kennedy Presidential Library and Museum, Boston, 24; Richard B. Levine/Newscom, 26–27; Red Line Editorial, 37, 56; A. Ricardo/Shutterstock Images, 42; Tony Quinn/Icon Sportswire, 49; AP Images, 50–51; Laurent Gillieron/Keystone/AP Images, 52–53; Mark Von Holden/Glassdoor/AP Images, 58; Ahn Young-joon/AP Images, 64–65; © Roberto Fumagalli/Alamy Stock Photo, 71; Cliff Owen/AP Images, 74–75; Tom Williams/CQ Roll Call/AP Images, 77, 86–87; Carolyn Kaster/AP Images, 85; Richard Drew/AP Images, 92; Yui Mok/PA Wire URN:21753054/AP Images, 99

Editor: Mirella Miller
Series Designer: Maggie Villaume

Publisher's Cataloging-in-Publication Data

Names: Higgins, Melissa, author. | Regan, Michael, author.
Title: The gender wage gap / by Melissa Higgins and Michael Regan.
Description: Minneapolis, MN : Abdo Publishing, 2017. | Series: Special reports |
        Includes bibliographical references and index.
Identifiers: LCCN 2016945214 | ISBN 9781680783940 (lib. bdg.) |
        ISBN 9781680797473 (ebook)
Subjects: LCSH: Women--Social conditions--21st century--Juvenile literature. |
        Feminism--Juvenile literature.
Classification: DDC 361--dc23
LC record available at http://lccn.loc.gov/2016945214

CONTENTS

CHAPTER ONE

SHEDDING LIGHT
ON THE
WAGE GAP

I n late November 2014, the movie studio Sony

Pictures Entertainment was the victim of a major

computer breach. Hackers released four Sony films

onto the Internet before their official launch dates,

enabling anyone to download the movies free of

charge. According to the Federal Bureau of Investigation

(FBI), the hackers were thought to be from North Korea

and were angry at Sony for making the upcoming

comedy film *The Interview*, about an assassination

attempt on North Korean leader Kim Jong-un. Even

more troubling than the movie releases, the hackers

After the Sony hack, Amy Adams, *left*, and Jennifer Lawrence,
right, realized they had been paid less than their
male costars in *American Hustle*.

stole and made public internal Sony documents revealing employees' personal information, including actor contracts and pay.

Jennifer Lawrence, who starred in the box office hit *The Hunger Games* before she was signed to act in the Sony movie *American Hustle*, discovered in a leaked e-mail that she and her female *American Hustle* costar, Amy Adams, both received less money than the film's male stars, Bradley Cooper and Christian Bale, received. Cooper and Bale were each paid $2.5 million upfront, whereas Lawrence and Adams were each paid $1.25 million.[1] The men also contracted for more back-end points, which is a percentage of box office receipts after a movie is released. Lawrence and Adams each earned seven points, and the men earned nine points. Although a difference of two percentage points might not seem like much, *American Hustle*

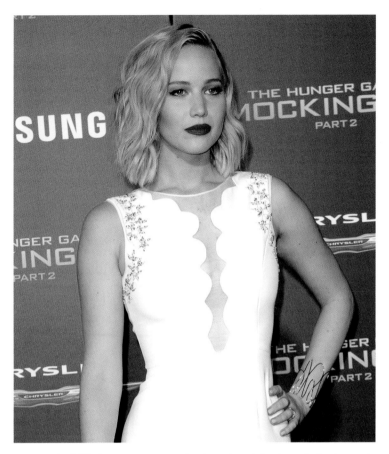

In 2013, Lawrence won an Academy Award for her role in the movie *Silver Linings Playbook.*

went on to earn $251 million worldwide, and those two percentage points became worth more than $5 million.[3]

As of August 2015, Lawrence had earned a total from all income sources of $52 million during the previous 12 months, making her the highest-paid female actor in the world.[4] She admitted she did not need the extra money. But having recently appeared in the huge hit

The Hunger Games, she was, arguably, the most famous and popular actor of her *American Hustle* costars. Lawrence shared her thoughts about the pay gap in an essay on actress Lena Dunham's online newsletter, *Lenny*. Lawrence wrote she was angry at the unfairness of being paid less than her male costars, and she was angry with herself for not being more assertive in asking for more. "I failed as a negotiator because I gave up early," she wrote. When closing her deal on *American Hustle*, she did not want to appear difficult or spoiled. Writing in her essay, Lawrence wondered whether all women are socially conditioned to be liked and not fight for what they deserve. "We've only been able to vote for what, 90 years? . . . Could there still be a lingering habit of trying to express our opinions in a certain way that doesn't 'offend' or 'scare' men?"[5]

"I'M OVER TRYING TO FIND THE 'ADORABLE' WAY TO STATE MY OPINION AND STILL BE LIKABLE!"[6]

—JENNIFER LAWRENCE, ACTRESS

After the Sony hack, Lawrence was determined to not undermine herself again. In 2015, she negotiated for a salary twice as large as her male costar, Chris Pratt, in her movie *Passengers*, another Sony picture. Sony attempted to renegotiate the deal and pay her less, but Lawrence threatened to walk out. The company agreed to her demands.

WHAT IS THE GENDER WAGE GAP?

The gender wage gap is an indicator of women's earnings compared with men's. It is figured by dividing the average annual earnings for women by the average annual earnings for men. According to the US Bureau of Labor Statistics, US women earned a little more than 78 cents for every dollar a man earned in 2015.[7] The gender wage gap exists in all occupations at all levels of employment in the United States.

It is important to keep in mind the 78-cent figure compares all working women with all working men, not women and men working in the same positions in the same industries. In that case, the gap shrinks—to as little as five cents, by some estimates. Because of this, some economists say the wage gap is a myth. Women earn less, on the whole, because of the choices they make, such as taking low-stress jobs in low-paying industries in exchange for more time at home to take care of their families.

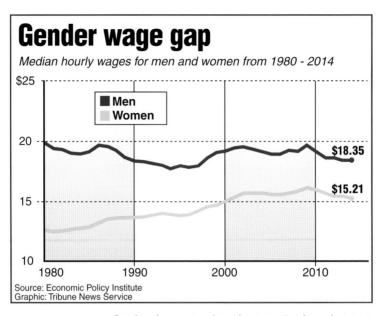

Gender wage gap

Median hourly wages for men and women from 1980 - 2014

Men
Women

$18.35

$15.21

$25
20
15
10

1980   1990   2000   2010

Source: Economic Policy Institute
Graphic: Tribune News Service

For decades, women have been earning less than men.

But where does that five-cent gap come from?
And what about women who work the same jobs as
men and are paid considerably less? Some scholars say
discrimination is to blame. The Sony leak, which revealed
Lawrence's pay gap with her male colleagues, also
revealed significant pay gaps between other male and
female Sony employees. A leaked spreadsheet showed a
female copresident of production at Columbia Pictures,
a division of Sony Pictures, made $1.5 million per year,
which was $1 million less than her male counterpart with
the same job title. The spreadsheet further showed that
of Sony's 17 employees making $1 million or more, only

one was a woman. Of all top-salaried Sony executives, 94 percent were male.[8]

Across many industries, women are poorly represented, or at least not represented at top pay levels. What isn't clear is the reason. Is it the choices women make? A lack of opportunity based on gender? A combination of different factors? Experts disagree.

"ULTIMATELY, WOMEN ARE BETTER OFF UNDERSTANDING THAT THEIR ACTIONS WILL LARGELY DETERMINE THEIR EARNINGS, RATHER THAN FEELING LIKE HELPLESS VICTIMS OF A SEXIST ECONOMY."[9]

—CARRIE LUKAS, MANAGING DIRECTOR OF THE INDEPENDENT WOMEN'S FORUM

PASSIONATE TOPIC

The gender wage gap brings up passionate beliefs because pay allows people to support themselves and their families. Work is an important part of life. The topic has been covered in the media and addressed by politicians ever since women joined the industry labor force in the mid-1800s. The US government began passing several fair wage and discrimination laws in 1938 to help protect all workers, including women. The most recent federal law—the Lilly Ledbetter Fair Pay Act of

2009—makes it easier for workers to challenge unequal pay. For solutions outside of government, experts look to the strategies of some US companies and even the US military to narrow the gap. These strategies include wage transparency, where pay rates are openly available for everyone to see, and not allowing pay negotiations. Lessons can also be learned from governments and businesses in foreign countries, where wage gaps are smaller than in the United States.

As with any passionate topic, controversy surrounds the gender wage gap. Not only is the gap measured in a misleading way, critics say, but women also need to take responsibility for their choices. It is women who choose to work fewer hours, in lower-paying industries, than men do. It is women who choose college majors in

WOMEN OF COLOR

Although the gender pay gap affects women of all races, the pay gap among women of color—Hispanic, American Indian, Native Hawaiian, and African American—is worse than the pay gap among white women. In 2014, the gap was widest among Hispanic women, who earned 54 percent of what white men earned. American Indian women earned 59 percent, Native Hawaiians earned 62 percent, and African American women earned 63 percent of white men's earnings. Asian American women had the lowest gap of all women, earning 90 percent of white men's earnings. The pay gap among white women in 2014 was 78 percent.[10]

lower-paying professions, such as teaching and social sciences. And it is women—such as Lawrence—who choose to not negotiate for higher pay. Whether the gender wage gap is large or small, no matter its causes, it will continue to raise accusations of unfairness for half of the US population.

SLOWLY CLOSING

Since 1963, the gender wage gap has been closing at an average rate of one-half of one cent per year. Based on data released by the US Census Bureau in 2015, some economists say the gap will close entirely in the United States by 2059. Worldwide, closing the gap will take much longer. World Economic Forum leaders believe the gender wage gap will not close for all countries until 2133. Helping close the gap is the fact that more women are working. The total number of women in the global workforce rose by 250 million between 2005 and 2015.[11]

CHAPTER TWO

BATTLING FOR
EQUAL PAY

F or both men and women, the workplace has centered on the home for much of human history. Tasks were often divided by gender—women cooked and wove, for example, whereas men worked in the fields—but jobs sometimes overlapped. The workshops of craftspeople and artisans were often connected to the home. The sense of shared responsibility and income between the sexes changed in the 1800s with the Industrial Revolution.

1800s: POOR WAGES AND WORKING CONDITIONS

The harnessing of electricity and the adoption of inventions such as the steam engine and sewing

In the 1800s, working conditions in factories were poor, and both men and women often worked 12 to 14 hours per day, six days per week, for low pay.

machine led to the US Industrial Revolution in the mid-1800s. For the first time, men and women began working in jobs away from home in great numbers. By the beginning of the 1900s, women made up approximately one-quarter of the industrial workforce. Men made the equivalent of approximately $13,000 per year in 2016 dollars. Male immigrants earned less, and women earned half, or around $6,500 per year, in 2016 dollars.[1] Conditions were even worse for black southern women, recently freed from slavery at the end of the American Civil War in 1865. They generally took jobs as farm laborers, household servants, and laundresses, often earning less than ten dollars per month.

Working conditions were so harsh that female workers—including launderers, cigar makers, printers, typographers, shoe stitchers, and bookbinders—organized into labor unions. Labor unions are associations of workers that promote labor rights and fair pay. Unions tried to negotiate for better wages and treatment, and they called for strikes when negotiating did not work. Strikes were not always successful, but some at least caught the public's attention. An unsuccessful work stoppage in 1883 by women at Western Union Telegraph Company, for example, gained nationwide attention when it brought communications in the United States to a standstill. African-American women formed the Washerwomen's Association of Atlanta in 1881. The women went on strike, demanding higher wages per pound of laundry. The strikers were forced to back down when the city threatened to charge them a $25 business license fee, but the union's efforts almost resulted in a general strike, which would have shut down the city.

A FAMOUS UNION ORGANIZER

One of most active union organizers for women in the 1800s was better known for promoting women's voting rights. Susan B. Anthony, born in Massachusetts in 1820, published a newsletter called *The Revolution*, which advocated for equal pay for equal work and an eight-hour workday. In 1868, she formed the Working Women's Association, a union for women typesetters and seamstresses not allowed to join men's unions. During a strike by male printers in New York, Anthony encouraged printing companies to hire women and pay them the same amount that men received. Men's unions said she was a strikebreaker and an enemy of labor. She died in 1906.

EARLY 1900s: WAGE LEGISLATION

Women's organizing and labor struggles continued into the 1900s. The Women's Trade Union League formed in 1903 to help women gain admission to men's trade unions, and female shirtmakers in New York conducted a strike against sweatshop conditions in 1909. In 1911, after a hard-fought battle with the New York Board of Education, female teachers in that state were given the same pay as male teachers. Federal and state governments enacted some labor laws, but the laws were either too weak to have an effect or were struck down by the US Supreme Court.

In 1938, President Franklin D. Roosevelt signed the Fair Labor Standards Act (FLSA) as part of his New Deal programs. He said he sought "legislation to end starvation wages and intolerable hours."[2] The act provided a 25-cent hourly minimum wage and a 44-hour workweek, and it eliminated most child labor. In 1940, the FLSA was amended and raised the minimum wage to 40 cents and lowered the workweek to 40 hours. The bill applied only to workers in unionized industries and left out workers in

agricultural or domestic jobs.

Labor unions lobbied to exclude women from unionized industrial jobs. One reason for excluding women was the societal belief that if a man earned enough money for his family, married women should leave their jobs and take care

"[THE FAIR LABOR STANDARDS ACT IS] THE MOST FAR-REACHING, FAR-SIGHTED PROGRAM FOR THE BENEFIT OF WORKERS EVER ADOPTED IN THIS OR ANY OTHER COUNTRY."[4]

—PRESIDENT FRANKLIN D. ROOSEVELT, 1938

of their households and raise children. This was especially

the case during the Great Depression of the 1930s,

when unemployment skyrocketed. Men, and even many

middle-class married women, argued that if women would

leave the workforce, men could then take those jobs and

unemployment would go down. But women of all races

and ethnicities continued to work out of necessity.

WARTIME

Wages for US women got a boost during both World

Wars. In World War I (1914–1918), the National War Labor

Board said women should be paid the same as men if they

worked in jobs usually held by men. In 1942, the National War Labor Board issued a similar order urging employers to pay women the same as men "for comparable quality and quantity of work on the same or similar operations."[5] Because the order was voluntary, not all employers followed it. Regardless of pay, with 16 million men serving in the US armed forces, women took positions in munitions factories, the aircraft industry, and other manufacturing industries normally held by men. Government-sponsored childcare gave mothers the opportunity to work. In 1945, women made up 34 percent of the US workforce, up from 28 percent in 1940. It was the biggest percentage increase of women in the US labor force in the 1900s.

After World War II (1939–1945), federal and local policies allowed employers to replace female workers with men. Many companies that had employed women now hired only men. As a

"WOMAN'S WORK"

At the beginning of World War I, the United States Employment Service (USES) published a list of jobs in manufacturing industries—such as munitions, toolmaking, metal products, and railway equipment—suitable for women. The USES officially designated these jobs as "woman's work" to shame men currently working in those positions to join the military. In some cases, women were even offered the same rate of pay as men.

result, many married women returned to their traditional roles as homemakers, and the percentage of all women in the workforce dropped back to 28 percent. Men's wages in most industries rose by almost 20 percent after World War II, and for the first time in US history, many families were able to live on a single income. But women continued to work. By 1953, the percentage of women in the workforce had grown to as high as it had been during World War II. Although women of color had long raised families while also contributing to household income, more white women were now taking on these two jobs.

1960s TO 2000— DISCRIMINATION ADDRESSED

Although men's and women's wages rose after World War II, a big gap remained. In 1960, women made an average of 61 cents for every dollar a man made.[6] In addition, the cultural expectation at the time was that white women should drop out of the labor force when they had children. This meant women were often hired for only temporary low-paying jobs rather than full-time careers.

MORE TO THE
STORY

1950s MOMS

Many women became traditional homemakers after World War II when men returned to the workforce. But cultural norms also played a role in why women stopped working. One was the Cold War—a cultural battle between US capitalism and Soviet Union communism. US propaganda showed the ideal woman as delicate, feminine, and tending to the family and home. Soviet women, on the other hand, were brawny, toiled in dingy factories, and placed their children in day care centers. US women were encouraged to live up to their country's patriotic ideal.

For young white women, the prime cultural theme in US life in the 1950s was having a husband. Many young women married immediately after high school, and women who did go to college were often said to be seeking a husband. A woman was considered an old maid if she was not engaged by at least her early 20s. The media, including television programs such as *Leave It to Beaver*, in which moms spent their days cleaning and cooking, further enforced the stereotype of the devoted stay-at-home mom. Women who wanted to break away from rigid gender roles and go to work were often mocked as being unhappy and manly.

Since the early 1950s, several bills had been introduced in Congress seeking equal pay for women, but all failed to move forward. In 1961, President John F. Kennedy formed a commission to study women and labor issues. The study resulted in an amendment to the FLSA called the Equal Pay Act. The act "prohibits sex-based wage discrimination between men and women in the same establishment who perform jobs that require substantially equal skill, effort and responsibility under similar working conditions."[7] The US Chamber of Commerce and retail merchant groups opposed the act. They argued that female workers were more expensive than male workers because women were frequently absent, quit more often then men, and needed separate bathrooms. Also, many states required longer rest periods and meal breaks for women. Even with these objections, the bill passed in 1963. As a result of the act, by 1971, employers were forced to pay more than $26 million in back wages to 71,000 women who were able to prove they were victims of wage discrimination.

In 1964, a provision of the Civil Rights Act—named Title VII—made any kind of discrimination based on race, religion, skin color, or gender illegal. Both the Civil

Rights Act and the Equal Pay Act contributed to women's sense of empowerment and promoted the idea that women belonged in the workplace rather than solely at home. Women continued joining the labor force and, by 1969, 36 percent of all US workers were women, compared with 34 percent in 1945. Forty percent of married women were working.[8] Women had made huge progress finding jobs, but although the Equal Pay Act attempted to address the most obvious forms of workplace bias, subtler drivers of pay inequality remained.

OTHER WORKPLACE WINS FOR WOMEN (AND MEN)

In addition to the Equal Pay Act and Title VII of the Civil Rights Act, the US Congress passed laws throughout the mid- and late 1900s to protect workers in all aspects of employment. This included hiring, pay, promotion, job assignment, and firing. One law was the Age Discrimination in Employment Act of 1967, which prohibits job discrimination against workers 40 years or older. The Pregnancy Discrimination Act of 1978 prohibits job discrimination against employees who are pregnant. In 1990, the Americans with Disabilities Act was passed, prohibiting job discrimination based on disability. The Family and Medical Leave Act of 1993 allows parents to take time off for family and medical reasons, such as for the birth or care of a child or to care for a seriously ill spouse.

President John F. Kennedy signs the Equal Pay Act as members of the American Association of University Women look on.

CHAPTER THREE

FACTORS AFFECTING THE WAGE GAP

The wage gap is computed by averaging what all women, working full time, earn in one year compared with what all men, working full time, earn in one year. In 2015, the figure commonly used was 78 cents. In other words, for every dollar a man made, a woman made 78 cents. Some experts say the reason for the difference in pay is gender discrimination—employers prefer male workers and pay them more than women. Others say it is a matter of social norms, work experience, the choices women make, or a

The wage gap still exists, and many men and women are working to end it through legislation.

INTERNATIONAL
TO THE
WAGE GAP
SAYS
WAGE
equal
pay
day ,-
equal
pay
day ,-

combination of many issues. Others say the real wage gap is so small, it does not exist.

JOB SEGREGATION: THE JOBS GAP

The 78-cent wage gap does not compare women and men working in the same positions. In fact, men and women tend to hold different kinds of jobs, often segregated by gender. Approximately 41 percent of all working women work in industries occupied mostly by women, whereas approximately 49 percent of all working men work in industries occupied mostly by men. In 2011, women made up 95.7 percent of secretaries and administrative assistants, 92.5 percent of receptionists, 90.5 percent of registered nurses, and 87 percent of other health-care workers or health aides.[1] Women also made up the majority of schoolteachers. On average, jobs in mostly male industries—such as construction, mechanics, engineering, police work, and firefighting—pay more than jobs in mostly female industries.

But even working the same jobs, there is a gap between what employers pay men and women. In the ten top occupations for women—including administrative

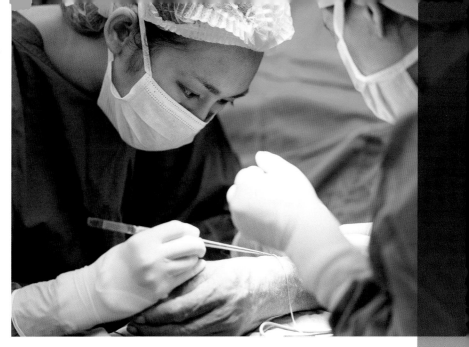

The wage gap actually increases for women in high-paying positions, such as business chief executives, lawyers, financial advisers, physicians, and surgeons.

assistants, secretaries, nurses, cashiers, and teachers—men are all paid more, on average, than women. The US Bureau of Labor Statistics tracks 534 occupations, and in only seven—including stock clerk and respiratory therapist—are women paid more than men, and these jobs employ only 3 percent of the entire full-time female workforce.[2]

SOCIAL AND ECONOMIC THEORIES

Experts point to many reasons for wage inequality. Some sociologists say women tend to gravitate toward jobs and careers that rely on traditional—and stereotyped—female

roles of nurturing, service, and supporting others.
Men, on the other hand, are drawn toward jobs that
support stereotypical male traits such as independence,
ambitiousness, and competitiveness. These stereotypes
tend to enforce the belief that women are inferior to
men and that men deserve more pay than women. Many
men and women buy into this belief, even if they do not
realize it.

Two economic theories—human capital theory and
discrimination theory—explain the wage gap in different
ways. Human capital theory says the wage gap is a result
of women's choices. For all workers, male or female, this
theory says a person's pay is based on personal traits
such as age, training, education, work experience, and
length of time in the workforce. If a new employee has
less education, training, or job experience than another
employee, he or she will be paid less. This theory also
suggests women choose jobs in industries that pay less
because they want more flexibility to take care of other
responsibilities, such as families.

Discrimination theory, in contrast, says the pay gap is
a result of bias on the parts of employers. Whether they

are aware of it or not, employers prefer men; men receive better evaluations and pay raises, both during the hiring process and after an employee is hired. For example, a 1997 study published by the National Bureau of Economic Research found that female musicians auditioning for a symphony orchestra were more likely to be hired if they performed behind a screen that hid their identities. A 1996 study published in the *Quarterly Journal of Economics* found that high-end restaurants in Philadelphia, Pennsylvania, hesitated in offering job interviews or server positions to women applicants, even if they were as well qualified as male applicants.

Some economists say both theories affect the wage gap. A 1997 study by economists Francine Blau and Lawrence Kahn showed 41 percent of the gender pay gap was due to discrimination. The rest was due

BLIND AUDITIONS

Research has shown people apply different standards when comparing men and women. Even if employers think they are being fair and equal, hidden biases influence decision-making. In 1970, women made up only 5 percent of all musicians in the top five US orchestras. In the 1970s and 1980s, many orchestras began using blind auditions, in which candidates perform behind a screen so their gender is not known. Using blind auditions, women had a 50 percent greater chance of being hired. As of 2014, women made up approximately half of many US orchestras, and in some case more than half.[3]

to a person's individual traits, such as job experience and total time in the workforce.

CHOICES AND EDUCATION

Critics of the human capital theory question the weight it places on women's choices. For example, the idea that women trade high-paying jobs for more flexible low-paying jobs is not true, critics say, because workers in low-paying jobs tend to have little control over their working hours and schedules. Workers in higher-paying positions have much more flexibility and control. They are also less likely to lose their jobs or miss out on chances to advance if they take advantage of family-friendly leave policies.

Critics also find fault with the theory's emphasis on more education leading to more pay. Every year since 1981, women have earned more bachelor's degrees than men have earned. Yet even when women graduate from college and start professional careers—including high-level careers in law, medicine, and business—they still earn less than men, both at the beginnings of their careers and through time. A study by the American Association of

University Women conducted in 2012 found an 82 percent difference in earnings between men and women one year after they graduated from college. A gap existed even among male and female graduates who entered the same occupations, especially engineering, computer science, business, and teaching. A 2012 study published by the UCLA Anderson School of Management found that female doctors would have been better off financially if they had become physician assistants—a career that pays less than doctors but requires less education and has lower upfront college costs. The same was not true for men.

"WOMEN ON AVERAGE ARE PUT IN SITUATIONS EVERY DAY THAT FOR A VARIETY OF REASONS MEAN THEY EARN LESS. MUCH OF WHAT WE NEED TO DO TO CLOSE THAT GAP IS TO CHANGE THE CONSTRAINTS THAT WOMEN FACE."[4]

—BETSEY STEVENSON, UNIVERSITY OF MICHIGAN'S GERALD R. FORD SCHOOL OF PUBLIC POLICY

HOME CARE AND CHILDCARE

In both of the 2012 earnings studies cited, women worked fewer hours than men, on average. In fact, women who have full-time jobs work an average of 35 minutes less at their jobs per day than men do. The difference is often linked to the amount of time women spend on home care and childcare—approximately 47 minutes more per day than men, in households with children younger than the age of six, and 22 minutes more per day if children are older.[5] Evidence shows that although working less does play a part in the wage gap, it is not a complete answer. In some high-paid professions, such as law and business, women who work fewer hours than men are paid much less than men—more than their actual loss of hours should reflect.

Although some human capital theorists would say women choose to work less in exchange for less pay, working fewer hours for many US women is a necessity. In 2015, 24 percent of all children in the United States lived with a single mother, whereas only 4 percent lived with a single father.[6] Discrimination theorists

EDUCATED WOMEN

Economists who say a lack of education should not be used as a reason for the wage gap point to the fact that women are earning more college degrees than ever before. Every year since 1981, more US women than US men have earned bachelor's degrees. In 2014, 32 percent of all US women had a bachelor's degree or higher, compared with 31.9 percent of all men—the first year that women with degrees outnumbered men with degrees.[7] One reason given for why women have pulled ahead of men is that in middle and high schools, girls spend more time on homework, are more organized, and are better at staying on task—important traits for succeeding in college.

say employers see mothers as being less dedicated to their jobs after they have children, because employers assume their kids and home lives come first. This can result in smaller and fewer pay raises for women than for men. On the other hand, men tend to get pay increases after becoming fathers, because employers see them as the family's main breadwinner, even if the man's wife also works full time. This is called the fatherhood bonus.

THE PROBLEM WITH NEGOTIATING

Negotiating can be tough for many women. However, it does not always bring the same results for women as it does for men. In a 2005 study, women read the same script as men while negotiating for salaries. Viewers of the negotiations approved of the men's negotiating style, but the women were seen as too demanding.

Acting too feminine can make women seem like pushovers, but being too aggressive can make them seem unlikable. One solution is to get rid of salary negotiations altogether, a change that women in all professions would likely benefit from.

FROM THE
HEADLINES

IS THE WAGE GAP A MYTH?

Some economists argue the gender wage gap is a myth, because comparing men and women in different careers with different work experiences is similar to comparing apples and oranges. A 2016 study by Glassdoor, a labor market research firm, tried to make an apples-to-apples comparison by adjusting for individual differences. They invited people who visited their website to share their job, wage, and other personal information, letting researchers gather data from hundreds of thousands of people in five countries—the United States, the United Kingdom, Australia, Germany, and France. By accounting for differences in experience, education, industry, and job, the wage gap in the United States shrank from 76 cents to 95 cents. In other words, women working in the same jobs as men, with the same education and experience, earned 5 percent less than men earned. The Glassdoor study also found the biggest cause of the wage gap was the so-called jobs gap, in which women and men tend to take jobs in industries that pay differently.

	UNADJUSTED GENDER PAY GAP		ADJUSTED GENDER PAY GAP	
Country	Average Female Pay per Male Pay	Percent Gap Between Female and Male Pay	Average Female Pay Per Male Pay	Percent Gap Between Female and Male Pay
United States	$0.76/$1	24.1 percent	$0.95/$1	5.4 percent
United Kingdom	£0.77/£1	22.9 percent	£0.95/£1	5.5 percent
Australia	AUD$0.83/$1	17.3 percent	AUD$0.96/$1	3.9 percent
Germany	€0.78/€1	22.5 percent	€0.95/€1	5.5 percent
France	€0.86/€1	14.3 percent	€0.94/€1	6.3 percent

Although the Glassdoor data showed that the adjusted wage gap was much less than the overall wage gap between men and women, it did not completely disappear. "It is remarkable that a significant gap persists even after we compare male-female worker pay at the job title and company level," wrote Andrew Chamberlain, one of the study's designers.[8] He did not provide a theory for the remaining gap.

CHAPTER FOUR

ENTERTAINMENT
AND SPORTS

T he gender wage gap may be most visible in industries such as entertainment and sports, where men and women do essentially the same jobs but often for different pay. Unlike some industries where women may not have a voice, when female celebrities and sports figures talk about a wage gap, the news media tends to pay attention.

MOVIES

Jennifer Lawrence became the face of the Hollywood gender wage gap in 2014 when she learned she had been paid less than her male costars in the movie *American Hustle*. That year, she and three other actresses

Meryl Streep is another actress enraged by what she sees as sexism in Hollywood.

made more than $20 million, whereas 21 actors made $20 million or more. Top actresses can earn between $10 million and $20 million per film and negotiate for part of a film's profits.[1] But few films have female main characters that warrant the high pay male actors receive for starring in popular movies with high commercial success. Of the 100 top-grossing films in 2014, women had the leads or coleads in only 21 of them. Wage gap critics view this disparity as a function of economics, not gender discrimination. Films with male leads bring in more income for movie studios, so those actors should naturally receive more pay.

But what happens when—as Lawrence discovered—actresses costar with men in the same movie and are still paid less? Three-time Academy Award winner Meryl Streep, who has more Oscar nominations than anyone else in history, said in an interview that she continues to receive less pay than her male costars. "Women's films don't sell, they tell you," she said in an interview. "There is this ancient wisdom that is difficult to move. . . . [Women] should all be included, we are half of the human race."[2]

The Hollywood gender wage gap is not only between actors and actresses but also in the film industry as a whole. Men hold most top positions. In 2014, women directed only 7 percent of the top 250 films. That same year, 22 percent of screenwriters were women, as were 20 percent of editors and 12 percent of cinematographers. In one note of progress, 33 percent of producers in 2014 were women.[3]

Grievances filed by the American Civil Liberties Union addressing discrimination against female directors caught the attention of the federal Equal Employment Opportunity Commission (EEOC). The EEOC—which enforces federal laws related to employment discrimination—began interviewing female filmmakers at the end of 2015 to find out if the commission should take legal action against film and television studios. As of May 2016, no report by the EEOC

HIGHEST-PAID ACTRESSES

In 2015, the ten highest-paid US actresses were Jennifer Lawrence ($52 million); Scarlett Johansson ($35.5 million); Melissa McCarthy ($23 million); Jennifer Aniston ($16.5 million); Julia Roberts ($16 million); Angelina Jolie ($15 million); Reese Witherspoon ($15 million); Anne Hathaway ($12 million); Kristen Stewart ($12 million); and Cameron Diaz ($11 million).[4] In contrast, the highest-paid male actor in 2015, Robert Downey Jr., made $80 million.[5]

Katy Perry is among the highest paid musicians in the world.

had been made public. Another report, published in 2016 by the Media, Diversity, and Social Change Initiative at the University of Southern California's Annenberg School for Communication and Journalism, gave failing grades to every movie studio and most television makers for an "epidemic of invisibility" for women, minorities, and lesbian, gay, bisexual, and transgender (LGBT) people.[6]

MUSIC

There is no doubt that women have found success in the music industry. In 2015, Katy Perry topped *Forbes* magazine's World's Highest Paid Musicians list. The $135 million she earned in 2015 made her the third-highest-paid celebrity in the world—male or female—after boxers Floyd Mayweather and Manny Pacquiao. Taylor Swift came in fourth on the Highest Paid Musicians list, making $80 million in 2015. But the larger list revealed a gap—there were only six women in the top 30, and two of them played in the same group—Stevie Nicks and Christine McVie of Fleetwood Mac. Lady Gaga and Beyoncé rounded out the six women in the top 30, earning $59 million and $54.5 million, respectively.[7]

BRAGGING OR INSPIRING?

When *Forbes* magazine asked Katy Perry to be on the cover of its 2015 highest-paid musicians issue, she wondered if it would look like she was flaunting her success or bragging. She decided to do the cover anyway, writing on her Instagram page, "Ladies, there is a difference between being humble and working hard to see the fruits of your labor blossom and your dreams realized. Hopefully this cover can be an inspiration to women out there that it's okay to be proud of hard earned success and that there is no shame in being a boss."[8]

Not only do female musicians, as a group, earn less than male musicians, but the majority of top musical acts are male. In a 2015 study of 12 summer music festivals in the United Kingdom, 86 percent of the performers were men. Some industry insiders do not have a problem with the imbalance, saying it is a matter of supply and demand—people want to see and hear certain musicians, and most of those musicians happen to be men. "Trust me," festival booker Melvin Benn told the *Guardian* newspaper, "if there was a female headline act in the rock genre that sold the same amount of tickets as any one of the headline acts this year, I'd book them. Why isn't there a heavy metal act like Metallica that is female? I can't answer that." Others believe the male-dominated music industry and a lack of promotion of women musicians are to blame. "It's important that we have women at the top as well as men, but we also need those female artists to be pushed through—by record companies, radio and the media," Emily Eavis, a festival booker, told the *Guardian*.[9]

Similar to the movie industry, men mostly control the music business. In *Billboard* magazine's 2016 Billboard Power 100 list, which ranks the most influential people in the music industry, women made

"I THINK THERE'S STILL AN UNDERLYING PERCEPTION THAT BEING CLASSICALLY 'GIRLY' AND KNOWING A LOT ABOUT MUSIC ARE MUTUALLY EXCLUSIVE. YOU SEE IT IN THE WAY PEOPLE TALK ABOUT 'GIRL-BANDS' AS IF THEY WERE SOMEHOW ABLE TO HEROICALLY OVERCOME THEIR FEMININITY AND PLAY MUSIC DESPITE BEING WOMEN."[10]

—ALYSSA DEHAYES, RIOT ACT MEDIA & ARROWHAWK RECORDS

up only 9 percent of the list. Music insiders note that more women work in middle-management positions, and it will take time for them to work their way up through the male-dominated ranks.

SPORTS

In 1972, the United States passed Title IX—which requires equal treatment for men and women in all educational programs that receive federal funding, including sports— into law. Since then, women's sports have blossomed, with both good news and bad in terms of wage equality. The major worldwide running marathons held in New York, New York; Boston, Massachusetts; London, England; Tokyo, Japan; Berlin, Germany; and Chicago, Illinois, offer the women's and men's winners the same prize money. The World Surf League gives equal prize money to men and

IS MEN'S TENNIS MORE POPULAR THAN WOMEN'S?

In March 2016, the survey company OnePulse asked 1,000 people in the United Kingdom whether female tennis players should earn the same as male tennis players. Seventy-eight percent of respondents said women should earn the same as men, whereas 14 percent said men should earn more, and 8 percent were unsure. When asked which type of matches they would rather watch, 24 percent of respondents said men's, 11 percent said women's, and 42 percent said they had no preference. Twenty-three percent of people said they would not go to a tennis match all.

women on the Championship Tour. In 1973, the US Open tennis tournament began paying women the same prize money as men. The rest of the world's three major tennis tournaments—called the Grand Slam events—eventually followed suit, making tennis one of the highest-paying sports for women.

Although the Grand Slam events may offer equal pay, tennis also provides an example of wage inequality. In smaller professional tournaments—which both male and female pros need to play in order to move up to bigger contests—women, on average, earn 77 cents for every dollar male tennis players earn. Wage gaps can also be found in other sports. The total prize money for the 2014 Professional Golf Association (PGA) tour was $340 million, more than five times the $61.6 million for the Ladies Professional Golf Association (LPGA) tour. The minimum salary for a Women's National Basketball Association (WNBA) player in 2015 was $38,900 and the maximum was $109,500. For National Basketball Association (NBA) players, the minimum salary was $525,000 and the maximum was $16.4 million. The US women's soccer team was paid $2 million for winning the 2015 Women's World

MORE TO THE
STORY

CONTROVERSY IN
WOMEN'S TENNIS

In March 2016, a controversy put a bright spotlight on discrimination in women's tennis. Raymond Moore, chief executive of the Indian Wells tennis tournament, said the Women's Tennis Association was lucky, because it "rides on the coattails" of men's tennis. "If I was a lady player," Moore said, "I'd go down every night on my knees and thank God that [men's tennis stars] Roger Federer and Rafa Nadal were born, because they have carried this sport." Male tennis player Novak Djokovic agreed with Moore, adding that men deserved more money because they drew more spectators. Djokovic added that he thought women faced more challenges than men faced to succeed in the game, including having to deal with "hormones."

Reacting to Moore's comments, women's tennis star Serena Williams said, "I think those remarks are very much mistaken and very, very, very inaccurate. Last year the women's final at the US Open sold out well before the men. I'm sorry, did Roger [Federer] play in that final or Rafa [Nadal] or any man play in a final that was sold out before the men's final? I think not."[1] Moore later apologized for his remarks.

Cup, whereas the US men's soccer team, which finished in eleventh place, received $9 million. The 2014 winning men's team from Germany took home $35 million.

People point to different reasons for the gender wage gap in sports, including the lack of players' unions, less interest and demand for tickets to women's matches, and less television revenue. If women's sports make less money, critics argue, why should they be paid the same as men? Discrimination has also been offered as an explanation. "It's a broader, more societal issue about the value of women in society," Karen Farquharson, associate dean at Swinburne University of Technology told *Forbes* magazine. "Society is patriarchal and male dominated, sports in particular. Sport is controlled by men."[12] Many of the same issues that affect the gender wage gap in entertainment and sports affect women's wages in other industries as well.

"PAYING MEN MORE FOR THE SAME SPORT GIVES WOMEN IN THE SPORT LESS INCENTIVE TO PUSH THEMSELVES AND DISCOURAGES FUTURE FEMALE PARTICIPATION IN THE SPORT."[13]

—WOMEN'S SPORTS FOUNDATION WEBSITE

The WNBA is yet another professional sport in which women are paid less than men for doing the same job.

FROM THE HEADLINES

WAGE DISCRIMINATION IN WOMEN'S SOCCER

In March 2016, five top players on the US women's national soccer team filed a wage-discrimination complaint with the EEOC against US Soccer, the governing body for men's and women's professional soccer in the United States. The players—Carli Lloyd, Becky Sauerbrunn, Alex Morgan, Megan Rapinoe, and Hope Solo—said members of the men's team were paid more, even though the women's team was more popular and brought in

more television revenue than the men's team. "The numbers speak for themselves," women's goalkeeper Solo told the *New York Times.* "We are the best in the world, have three World Cup championships, four Olympic championships. . . . [the men] get paid more to just show up than we get paid to win major championships." The women players said they were paid approximately 40 percent of what male players were paid. The player's lawyer, Jeffrey Kessler, said, "This is the strongest case of discrimination against women athletes in violation of law that I have ever seen."[14]

In a 2016 statement, US Soccer said all players through the women's player's union agreed on women's salaries and bonuses. In May 2016, US Soccer asked the EEOC to dismiss the players' complaint. No one was sure how long it would take the EEOC to make a decision. If successful, the women's players could receive millions of dollars in back pay.

Carli Lloyd, Alex Morgan, Megan Rapinoe, Becky Sauerbrunn, and Hope Solo, *left to right*, brought attention to the discrimination within the professional soccer community.

CHAPTER FIVE

OTHER
INDUSTRIES

With few exceptions, women are paid less than men in all industries and occupations. The gender wage gap goes all the way up the corporate ladder and stretches into the federal government. The gap shrinks when pay rates are made public and the gap is measured on the basis of job title rather than individual differences between workers.

BUSINESS

Women are thriving in business. In 2015, women made up 51 percent of management and professional jobs in the United States. But a 2016 survey by the online jobs site CareerBuilder.com found that one in five human resource managers admitted women at their companies

Marissa Mayer is one of the few female CEOs of a large corporation, yet she still makes less than her male counterparts.

earned less than men doing the same work. They said men at their companies were approximately three times more likely to earn more than $100,000 and twice as likely to earn $50,000 or more.[1] According to the Bureau of Labor Statistics, the average weekly salary for a female manager in 2015 was $996, while a male manager's average weekly salary was $1,383.[2]

Compared to the large number of women in middle management, few women reach the top rungs of the corporate ladder. As of May 2016, only 20 women headed the top 500 companies included in *Fortune* magazine's Fortune 500. That was up from 1995, when there were no female chief executive officers (CEOs), but down from 24 female CEOs at the end of 2014. Since 1995,

A CONSERVATIVE VIEWPOINT

The Heritage Foundation, founded in 1973, is an educational and research institute that promotes conservative public policies such as free enterprise, limited government, and individual freedom. When it comes to the wage gap, the foundation follows the human capital theory that personal choices account for differences in pay between women and men. Further, the foundation believes the wage gap is closer to 95 cents than 77 cents. Romina Boccia, a policy analyst with the foundation, said in 2014, "Once key factors such as occupation, education, and length of service are taken into account, the wage gap in the federal workforce all but disappears. The same applies to the economy-wide gender pay gap."[3] The foundation believes misleading claims about the gender gap discourage women from making choices that would help them succeed.

approximately one new woman CEO joined the list every two years.[4]

Although most CEOs—including women—make salaries in the millions of dollars, men make more. In 2015, the combined yearly salaries of the two highest-paid male CEOs—David Zaslav of Discovery Communications and Leslie Moonves of CBS—was more than the combined salaries of the top ten female CEOs. A 2015 study by *Bloomberg* magazine found that female executives made approximately 18 percent less than male executives. A 2015 academic study by the Federal Reserve Bank of New York found that women made smaller bonuses and received smaller pay raises than men. The study also found that when companies did poorly, female executives took bigger losses than men. But when companies did well, men saw bigger bonuses than women did.

Experts offer several reasons why women executives do not earn as much as men

"IT'S NOT FAIR, AND IT'S NOT RIGHT, AND NOBODY REALLY MEANS IT, BUT YOU CAN SEE IN THE NUMBERS HOW IT COMES OUT. POLICY IS EASY. PERCEPTION AND EXPECTATIONS ARE HARD."[5]

—SALLIE KRAWCHECK, FORMER BANK OF AMERICA WEALTH MANAGEMENT PRESIDENT, REGARDING PENALTIES WOMEN EXECUTIVES FACE FOR PRIORITIZING THEIR FAMILIES

TOP CEOs AND THEIR SALARIES

HIGHEST-PAID FEMALE CEOs (2015)[6]	
Marissa Mayer, Yahoo	$42.1 million
Carol Meyrowitz, TJX Companies	$23.3 million
Margaret Whitman, Hewlett-Packard	$19.6 million
Indra Nooyi, PepsiCo	$19.1 million
Phebe Novakovic, General Dynamics	$19 million

HIGHEST-PAID MALE CEOs (2015)	
David Zaslav, Discovery Communications	$156.1 million
Leslie Moonves, CBS	$54.4 million
Philippe Dauman, Viacom	$44.3 million
Robert Iger, Walt Disney	$43.7 million
Leonard Schleifer, Regeneron Pharmaceuticals	$42 million

earn. The 2015 Federal Reserve Bank study found women negotiated less than their male counterparts, and they worked fewer hours due to family responsibilities. The study also found women were less likely to be part of their company's power structure. "Female top executives are less entrenched than male top executives, due to their younger age and their relative difficulties in accessing informal networks," the authors of the study concluded.[7] In other words, employers tended to support and promote people they were comfortable with and related to, and women had difficulty breaking into these mostly male networks.

INDUSTRIES WITH THE WIDEST AND NARROWEST GAPS

In 2015, Glassdoor.com studied what happened to the gender wage gap when it compared men and women with the same job title, similar education,

SHOULD WOMEN BE CEOs?

With so few women executives, it might seem the public does not believe women belong in the top tiers of business leadership. But a 2015 Pew Research report showed that 80 percent of US men and women did not consider gender an important quality in a business leader. Further, approximately one-third of those surveyed thought having more female leaders in business and government would be good for the country. But respondents also said it was easier for men to rise to the top than for women, and that some industries—such as oil and computer software—would do better with a man at the helm.

branches of military service. Wages are preset for every rank, and pay scales are public knowledge, so personnel can see whether they are being paid less than someone else doing the same job. There is also no negotiating salary, because pay is predetermined. If women want to exchange lower pay for more flexibility to take care of children, they cannot—a woman must work the same hours as her male colleagues or she has to leave the service. Soldiers and sailors, men and women alike, sometimes spend months away from their families.

But there is still an overall wage gap in the military, because fewer women occupy the upper ranks. In 2015, according to the US Department of Defense, women made up 7.9 percent of generals, 11.7 percent of colonels, 16.5 percent of majors, 19.4 percent of captains,

WOMEN EARNING MORE THAN MEN

The US Census Bureau gathers information on the annual salaries of men and women in 342 professions. In 2013, its data showed that women made slightly more than men made in the following nine occupations ("+" indicates how much more women made per year than men): producers and directors (+$3,800); wholesale and retail buyers, not farm equipment (+$1,400); vehicle and equipment cleaners (+$1,200); transportation security screeners (+$1,000); social and human service assistants (+$800); special education teachers (+$450); transportation, storage, and distribution managers (+$240); counselors (+$70); and dishwashers (+$30).[10]

and 20 percent of lieutenants. A study by the RAND

Corporation found that although 45 percent of white men

would become majors during their military careers, only

31 percent of white women would reach that rank. But

the RAND study also noted that the rate of promotions for

women in the military was still

much higher than for female

CEOs in private industry. And as

women began entering combat

positions in 2016, the number

of women in higher ranks

was expected to increase. For

example, in 2016, US Air Force

General Lori Robinson became

the first woman to head a US

combatant command.

GOVERNMENT

Similar to the military, the US

federal government uses a

structured pay system with

salary rates open to the public.

LEAN IN

In 2013, Sheryl Sandberg—CEO of Facebook—authored a book titled *Lean In*, about women becoming more involved in corporate leadership. "Leaning in" refers to women doing whatever it takes to succeed, including working extra hours and volunteering for difficult assignments, rather than giving up and "leaning back" or "leaning out." The book brought national attention to the issue of equality and the challenges women face in the workplace, and it soon became a movement. Although many women have benefitted from the *Lean In* philosophy, it also has its critics. They say corporate success and ambition are not always a good fit for all women, especially women who are also raising children. In May 2016, having been a single mom for a year after the death of her husband in 2015, Sandberg admitted her book should have better addressed the challenges faced by single mothers.

Most state and local governments do the same. Concerned about pay equity, President Barack Obama asked the US Office of Personnel Management (OPM) in 2013 to study the gender wage gap in the federal government. In 2014, OPM released its study, which found that women's starting salaries lagged behind men's by an average of 10 percent. Some of the difference was due to job segregation—more women than men filled lower-salary positions, whereas more men than women held higher-paying positions. Other factors contributing to the gap included women having less work experience, taking time off for caregiving, lower motivation and job performance, and possibly some discrimination. Overall, OPM found the gender pay gap in government to be 87 cents, ten cents less than the country as a whole. Conservatives used the report's findings to support their argument that the wage gap was not a problem and had nothing to do with discrimination.

To reduce the gap further, OPM asked federal agencies in 2015 to not consider an employee's previous salary history as the only factor in setting pay for new employees. OPM Director Beth Cobert wrote, "Reliance on existing salary to set pay could potentially adversely

The US government has a smaller gender wage gap than the private industry's, but a gap still exists.

affect a candidate who is returning to the workplace after having taken extended time off from his or her career, or for whom an existing rate of pay is not reflective of the candidate's current qualifications or existing labor market conditions."[11] Advocates for female government workers thought OPM's recommendations should have been made requirements.

CHAPTER SIX

A GLOBAL
PROBLEM

"**T**here is no country on earth where women are paid as much as men," Elaine Moore, a reporter for the London-based *Financial Times*, wrote in 2014.[1] The gender wage gap exists throughout the world and for many of the same reasons it persists in the United States. But the gap varies significantly, depending on where women live and on what steps governments and businesses are taking to close it.

GLOBAL GENDER WAGE GAP BY THE NUMBERS

In 2014, the Organization for Economic Co-operation and Development (OECD) reported a range in the

South Korea has one of the largest wage gaps, meaning women are earning low hourly wages in jobs such as factory positions.

gender pay gap between its 34 member countries from a low of 5.62 percent in New Zealand to a high of 36.6 percent in South Korea. The United States ranked twenty-third on the list. According to *The Global Gender Gap Report 2015*, published by the World Economic Forum, a woman's annual average salary worldwide in 2015 was $11,000, the same as a man's salary in 2006. Between 2006 and 2015, the average man's annual salary rose $10,000 (from $11,000 to $21,000), whereas the average woman's annual salary rose $5,000 (from $6,000 to $11,000).[2]

"UNLESS WE START CHANGING THE CULTURE AROUND THE DIVISION OF LABOUR AT HOME THERE'S ALWAYS GOING TO BE THAT EXTRA BURDEN ON WOMEN. . . . THAT MEANS WE'RE NOT GOING TO BE ABLE TO MAINTAIN THOSE HIGH LEVELS OF WOMEN JOINING THE WORKFORCE ALL THE WAY THROUGH TO MIDDLE MANAGEMENT AND SENIOR POSITIONS."[3]

—SAADIA ZAHIDI, LEAD AUTHOR OF *THE GLOBAL GENDER GAP REPORT 2015*

Although it might seem as though industrialized nations that promote democracy and equality would outrank developing countries in terms of gender pay, this is not always the case. Five of the 15 countries with the worst gender pay gaps on the OECD list—the Netherlands, Finland, Austria, the United Kingdom, and Portugal—are members

of the European Union (EU).
A 2010 EU study found that,
similar to the United States,
women in the EU's member
countries tended to segregate
into lower-paying jobs, were
hired less often than men for
high-level positions, and lost
pay due to childcare and a lack
of education and experience.
The study also found that fewer
women belonged to unions,
which negotiate on behalf of
employees for higher salaries
and benefits.

GLOBAL GENDER WAGE GAP RANKINGS

The World Economic Forum publishes global reports with the goal of improving the state of the world. *The Global Gender Gap Report 2015* ranked 145 countries on how well they were "leveraging their female talent pool." The ten countries with the smallest gender wage gaps in 2015 were Iceland, Norway, Finland, Sweden, Ireland, Rwanda, Philippines, Switzerland, Slovenia, and New Zealand. The United States was in twenty-eighth place. The ten countries with the widest wage gaps were Yemen, Pakistan, Syria, Chad, Iran, Jordan, Morocco, Lebanon, Mali, and Egypt.[5]

EFFORTS IN THE EU

Some European governments have stepped up programs
to target the gender wage gap. The United Kingdom,
for example, raised its minimum wage in 2016 from 6.70
to 7.20 British pounds (US $9.48 to $10.19), to increase to
9 British pounds (US $12.72) by 2020.[4]

In 2010, Finland's government—where 80 percent of the local public employees were women—began paying some women's salaries to make them more equal with men's. Finland also expanded family leave policies beneficial to women. Some business organizations in Italy, Sweden, the United Kingdom, and Germany have promoted family leave policies and increased opportunities for women in mostly male careers, such as construction and management.

INTERNATIONAL BILL OF RIGHTS FOR WOMEN

Since its adoption in 1979, only seven of the 193 member countries of the United Nations (UN) have not ratified the international bill of rights for women, known as the Convention on the Elimination of all forms of Discrimination Against Women (CEDAW). The 186 countries that have signed on have committed to ending discrimination against women, including low wages, sex trafficking, and gender violence. The United States has not ratified the CEDAW. Two-thirds of the US Senate must vote in favor of the CEDAW for it to be ratified, but it has never made its way to the Senate floor for a vote. The only other countries that have not ratified the international women's bill of rights are Iran, Sudan, South Sudan, Palau, Somalia, and Tonga.

SUB-SAHARAN AFRICA

A gender gap report issued in 2015 by the World Economic Forum identified sub-Saharan Africa, countries located south of the Sahara Desert, as having five of the top 15 countries with the lowest gender wage gaps. In Rwanda, 88 percent of women were employed

MORE TO THE STORY

A BRITISH TRANSPARENCY SUCCESS STORY

In 2015, the United Kingdom introduced a plan requiring companies with 250 or more employees to report gaps in gender pay. Prime Minister David Cameron said the disclosures "will cast sunlight on the discrepancies and create the pressure we need for change, driving women's wages up."[6] Opponents of the British plan said it was too expensive and too complicated. Others said it did not address problems such as women being blocked from higher-paying jobs and social problems such as unconscious bias.

PricewaterhouseCoopers, a global business consulting firm, decided to voluntarily publish its own gender wage gap analysis in 2015. The company found its 15 percent pay gap was the result of a lack of women in senior jobs and not promoting women fairly. Although women held 30 percent of jobs just below the partner level, only 16 percent were being promoted to partner. PricewaterhouseCoopers also discovered that men who were not promoted to partner were offered bonuses to keep them from quitting, whereas women who were passed over for promotion were not offered bonuses. Within a year, the company doubled the number of women partners and corrected other unfair practices that had contributed to the gender wage gap. PricewaterhouseCoopers proved the government's plan could work.

(compared with 66 percent of women in the United States), and 64 percent of the country's politicians were women (compared with 19 percent in the United States).

The success of women in some African countries can be traced to years of rebel uprisings and mass killings. In 1994, tired of their country's wars and male-biased policies, women in Rwanda banded together and demanded power. They called for equality in marriage and changed their country's constitution to require that women hold 30 percent of top positions in the government. Women put off having children and went to work. Alexandra Topping, a journalist for the *Guardian* newspaper, wrote, "A swath of laws have given women the right to inherit land, share the assets of a marriage and obtain credit. . . . Maternal mortality is lower and the birth rate is falling."[7]

ROOM TO IMPROVE: SOUTH KOREA AND JAPAN

South Korea, which has the fifteenth-largest economy in the world, ranks last among the 34 countries OECD included in its 2015 wage gap report. The World Economic Forum ranked South Korea number 115 of

Some South Korean and Japanese women who want to pursue careers are choosing to not marry or have children.

the 145 countries in its 2015 gender gap report. Women in South Korea faced a 44 percent difference in wages compared with South Korean men. Japan ranked as number 101 on the World Economic Forum list.

Working women in South Korea and Japan share similarities. In both countries, working long hours and then socializing after work are traditional parts of professional work life. Even though South Korean and Japanese women are as educated as men, the need for them to shoulder childcare responsibilities is even greater than in other countries, because their partners are rarely home to share those duties. Many more women work part time. In South Korea in 2013, more than 27 percent of women worked part time, compared with a worldwide average of 12.5 percent. According to the Korean Women's Development Institute, underemployed women are costing South Korea $13.3 billion annually in lost wages and education expenses.[8]

To combat this situation, the South Korean government is increasing the number of childcare facilities to support working mothers. In 2008, the nation began a Best Family Friendly Management program, which offers incentives to local government offices and businesses with family friendly policies. It is also increasing paternity leave benefits so men will take more responsibility at home. In Japan, where women account for 68 percent of all part-time and temporary employees, Prime Minister Shinzo Abe set a goal for women to hold 30 percent of all government and private sector leadership positions by 2020.

"OUR STRATEGY HAS BEEN TO CHANGE THE LAWS AND INSTITUTIONS FIRST SO THE REST OF THE SOCIETY CAN CATCH UP."[9]

—CHUNG BONG-HYUP, SOUTH KOREA'S DIRECTOR GENERAL AT THE MINISTRY OF GENDER EQUALITY

CHAPTER SEVEN

RECENT
WAGE GAP
LEGISLATION

A gender wage gap has existed in the United States since US women first joined the industrial workforce in the 1800s. Calls for the federal government to enforce equal pay have been made for just as long. The FLSA of 1938, the Equal Pay Act of 1963, and Title VII of the Civil Rights Act of 1964 have all helped promote pay equality. With one notable exception, wage-related laws have stagnated in the US Congress, leading the president and individual states to fill the legislative vacuum.

Former Senate Appropriations Committee Chair Senator Barbara Mikulski has been a fierce advocate for women and their rights.

THE PAYCHECK FAIRNESS ACT

Under current law, women who sue their employers for pay discrimination must prove gender bias. The Paycheck Fairness Act (PFA), which had not been passed as of 2016, would require companies to prove they are not discriminating against women by providing data to the EEOC on pay, hiring, firing, and promotion. The act would also prohibit companies from retaliating against workers who ask for or reveal information about wage information at their company.

The PFA, or some version of it, has been introduced in Congress every other year since 1997. In 2015, 43 of 44 Senate Democrats and all House Democrats in Congress signed on as sponsors of the House and Senate bills. Of Republicans,

1923 EQUAL RIGHTS AMENDMENT FAILS

In 1923, Alice Paul, a women's rights activist, wrote an equal rights amendment to the US Constitution. The heart of the amendment states, "Equality of rights under the law shall not be denied or abridged by the United States or any State on account of sex."[1] Congress finally passed the amendment in 1972 and sent it to individual states for ratification. In 1982, the amendment came close to passing when it was approved by 35 states. But because a constitutional amendment requires the approval of at least three-quarters of all states—or 38 states—it failed. The amendment has been reintroduced in every congressional session since 1982 but has never again made its way out of Congress.

only Representative Chris Smith of New Jersey signed on as a cosponsor. In support of the bill, Democratic Senator Barbara Mikulski said, "Equal pay is not just for our pocketbooks, it's about family checkbooks and getting it right in the law books. The PFA ensures that women will no longer be fighting on their own for equal pay for equal work."[2] Generally, Republicans have said the act would increase discrimination lawsuits and thereby increase costs to businesses. They have also said the legislation is simply a political ploy by Democrats to gain votes during election campaigns. Republican Senate Majority Leader Mitch McConnell said, "These are bills designed intentionally to fail so that Democrats can make campaign ads about them

House Minority Leader Nancy Pelosi, *third from left*, discusses the PFA in 2016.

failing."[3] The PFA came closest to being passed in 2009 when Democrats controlled both houses of Congress; it failed by only two votes.

LILLY LEDBETTER FAIR PAY ACT OF 2009

Lilly Ledbetter worked for the Goodyear Tire & Rubber Company for 19 years as an area manager. In 1998, only a few months before she retired, she received an anonymous note informing her she was being paid 40 percent less than the lowest-paid male area manager in the company. In 1998, Ledbetter filed a pay discrimination lawsuit under Title VII of the Civil Rights Act of 1964, and a jury awarded her back pay and $3.3 million in compensatory and punitive damages. Goodyear contested the jury award in the US Supreme Court, which reversed the lower court's ruling in 2007.

Ledbetter's case failed because of a stipulation of the Civil Rights Act that said any discrimination suit had to be filed within 180 days from

"IT IS FITTING THAT WITH THE VERY FIRST BILL I SIGN—THE LILLY LEDBETTER FAIR PAY ACT—WE ARE UPHOLDING ONE OF THIS NATION'S FIRST PRINCIPLES: THAT WE ARE ALL CREATED EQUAL AND EACH DESERVE A CHANCE TO PURSUE OUR OWN VERSION OF HAPPINESS."[4]

—PRESIDENT BARACK OBAMA, JANUARY 29, 2009

the first time an employer paid a woman less than what a man was paid for the same job. The deciding justices said Ledbetter failed to meet that deadline. Supreme Court Justice Ruth Bader Ginsburg, one of the dissenting justices in the five-to-four ruling, strongly suggested Congress take action to fix the 180-day clause in the Title VII law. Democratic legislators reacted quickly by introducing the Lilly Ledbetter Fair Pay Act in 2007. The act amended or modified four previous laws, including Title VII of the Civil Rights Act of 1964 and the Age Discrimination in Employment Act of 1967. Instead of limiting lawsuits to 180 days from the original instance of low pay, the 180 days would reset with each new paycheck.

LILLY LEDBETTER

Lilly Ledbetter was born in Possum Trot, Alabama, in 1938. In 1979, she applied for and was hired for a managerial position with the Goodyear Tire & Rubber Company, making her one of the first female managers ever hired at Goodyear. In 1998, she took an early retirement from the company and filed a discriminatory wage lawsuit after discovering she had been paid at least 40 percent less than men working at Goodyear in her same position. Though she received no award after the Supreme Court ruled against her case, the law in her name ensures that her ten-year fight will protect the equal pay rights for other US women. As of 2016, Ledbetter traveled throughout the United States, urging women and minorities to stand up for their civil rights.

The House of Representatives passed the bill, but it was then defeated in the Senate in 2008 when Senate Republicans used a filibuster to block the act from coming to a vote. Republicans generally opposed the act, saying the law would result in lawsuits meant to annoy or harass a company with little chance of winning in court. The act was reintroduced in the Senate in 2009. Five Republicans, a majority of Democrats, and two independents voted to prevent a filibuster, and the act passed. President Obama signed the Lilly Ledbetter Fair Pay Act on January 29, 2009. Since then, a number of discrimination lawsuits have progressed through the courts.

LACK OF PAID PARENTAL LEAVE LEGISLATION

According to the World Economic Forum, the United States is the only industrialized nation that does not have a national paid leave program for new parents. Only the states of California, Washington, and New Jersey have enacted parental leave laws. "[The United States'] policies on parental leave, sick leave, vacations, and other social programs such as childcare are considered substandard and ungenerous by many scholars who study comparative, international social policies," noted Re:Gender, a network of institutions and individuals working to end gender inequality.[5]

NATIONAL EQUAL PAY ENFORCEMENT TASK FORCE

In his 2010 State of the Union address, President Obama announced, "We're going to crack down on violations of equal pay laws—so that women get equal pay for an equal day's work."[6] He also established the National Equal Pay Task Force. It consisted of members from the EEOC, the Department of Justice, the Department of Labor, and the OPM.

The purpose of the task force was to study why women were not getting equal pay for equal work in agencies and companies that worked for the federal government. It also enforced equal pay. As a result of the task force's activities, the number of pay discrimination cases decided by the Office of Federal Contract Compliance Programs (OFCCP) nearly tripled from 2010 to 2013. During that time, the OFCCP decided 80 cases and recovered $2.5 million in back pay for approximately 1,200 employees. The OFCCP is a division of the US Department of Labor. It makes sure companies doing business with the government are obeying federal discrimination and affirmative action laws.

EQUAL PAY DAY

Every year since 1996, the National Committee on Pay Equity—a coalition of women's and civil rights organizations—has sponsored Equal Pay Day. It illustrates how far into the following year women would have to work to make up the difference, on average, between what women and men earn. In 2016, that day was April 12.

CONGRESSIONAL INACTION LEADS TO EXECUTIVE ORDERS AND STATE ACTION

Because so many US women segregate into low-paying industries, some economists consider the federal minimum wage to be one of the strongest weapons for decreasing the gender wage gap. As of 2016, the minimum wage was $7.25 per hour, which Congress set in 2009. In 2013, President Obama urged the US Congress to raise the minimum wage to help people—and especially women—afford the rising costs of food, housing, and transportation. As of 2016, minimum wage legislation had stalled in Congress.

Frustrated by the lack of progress on raising wages and narrowing the gender wage gap, Obama issued an executive order in 2014 prohibiting federal contractors—companies that provide goods and services to the federal government—from discriminating against employees who discuss their wages. He also ordered companies that contract with the federal government to pay a minimum wage of $10.10 per hour. In 2015, Obama required all federal contractors to provide one hour of paid sick leave for every 30 hours employees worked.

Several states have enacted their own minimum wage laws. Beginning in January 2017, the California minimum wage was set to rise from $10 per hour to $10.50 per hour for businesses with more than 26 employees. Companies with 25 employees or fewer would have until the following year to comply. The minimum wage would gradually rise to $15 per hour by 2023. Lawmakers in New York boosted the minimum wage in New York City from $9 to $15 per hour by 2019 for companies with more than 11 employees, and state suburbs would reach $15 per hour by 2022. In early 2016, Oregon raised its minimum wage from $9.75 to $14.75 per hour by 2022 in the Portland area and slightly lower in other parts of the state.

HOW LONG DO EXECUTIVE ORDERS LAST?

Executive orders can be issued by the president without the approval of Congress and have the effect of law. An order stays in effect until it is reversed, canceled, or replaced by the president who made the order or any following president. Congress can pass a law that bans an executive order. Also, the US Supreme Court can rule an executive order unconstitutional.

FROM THE HEADLINES

BUSINESSES REQUIRED TO REPORT SALARIES

In January 2016, as part of his efforts to reduce the gender wage gap, President Obama announced new rules that would require large companies in the United States to report salaries based on employee race, gender, and ethnicity. The EEOC would then be allowed to investigate and sue any company that paid women less than men, and any company named in an EEOC lawsuit would be made public. "The notion that we would somehow be keeping my daughters . . . any of your daughters out of opportunity, not allowing them to thrive in any field, not allowing them to fully participate in every human endeavor, that's counterproductive," Obama said during his announcement of the ruling.[7] The EEOC expected to publish its first report in September 2017 and hoped the data would help company managers decide how to set fair pay.

Business groups condemned the policy, saying the administration was overreaching its authority, the data would be hard to gather, and the rules placed too many burdens on employers.

Some critics did not think it would work. David Cohen, president of DCI Consulting Group, which conducts pay equity studies, said comparing employees in different jobs in different markets with

President Obama is greeted by Lilly Ledbetter before announcing his new efforts for fair pay.

different abilities did not make sense. "If the goal of this report is to raise awareness . . . that's great. If the goal is to use this report as a predictor of discrimination, it will fail," he told the *Washington Post*.[8]

CHAPTER EIGHT

HOW TO SHRINK
THE WAGE GAP

The gender wage gap has narrowed during the past 100 years, but it is far from disappearing. Many solutions have been recommended to close the gap, some of which are already being tried. Business practices, government policies, schools, and actions by women themselves all have a role to play in promoting equal pay.

MAKE WAGES TRANSPARENT AND ELIMINATE NEGOTIATING

Research has shown that gender discrimination can prevent women from being hired and keep them from receiving pay raises, bonuses, and promotions equal to men's. One way to address discrimination is through

Many people have worked tirelessly over the years to lessen the gender wage gap.

A Fair Shot *for* Women
to Make the Pay they Earn

77¢
for every dollar
a man makes

#F

wage transparency—making salary data openly available for all to see. When everyone knows what everyone else in a company is paid, then all workers can decide what is fair. In addition to lowering the gender wage gap, studies suggest transparency leads to greater employee satisfaction and less employee turnover.

> "NO BUSINESS WHICH DEPENDS FOR EXISTENCE ON PAYING LESS THAN LIVING WAGES TO ITS WORKERS HAS ANY RIGHT TO CONTINUE IN THIS COUNTRY."[1]
>
> —PRESIDENT FRANKLIN D. ROOSEVELT, 1933

A positive side effect of wage transparency is making salary negotiations unnecessary, because hiring salaries are based on the position, not the person. This is especially important for women, because studies have shown that negotiating can be difficult for women and might even backfire if employers think a woman is coming across as too aggressive. Ridding negotiating from hiring is already happening at a few companies, including the tech companies Google and Reddit. Rather than the common practice of basing starting salaries on what an employee earned at his or her previous job, Google and Reddit pay the same starting salaries to all employees with the same job descriptions. Google decides what the job is worth and bases salaries on the job's market value. This means some employees might see a drop in wages when they are hired. But, as Laszlo Bock, people operations chief at Google, told the *Washington Post*, "If you do that instead of starting from where somebody is today, the [wage gap] problem goes away."[2] A key to this strategy is not asking potential employees for their salary histories.

Many employers balk at making wages public. They worry workers will want more pay or angrily quit if they see what everyone else is making. Keeping wages secret helps companies control costs, and it also protects employee privacy. But the trend is toward greater transparency as younger

ACTIVIST SHAREHOLDERS DEMAND WAGE TRANSPARENCY

In early 2016, stock investment firm Arjuna Capital began pressuring technology companies to disclose their gender pay-gap figures. If the companies did not comply, Arjuna said it would take action to force the issue. By March 2016, Intel, Apple, Expedia, and Amazon had all revealed their wage data, and eBay, Facebook, Microsoft, and Google were considering it. Citigroup said creating such a report would be too costly and time consuming. Activist shareholders such as Arjuna are concerned about both equality and profits. "The technology industry lives and dies on innovation, and gender-diverse teams are shown to be a key factor," said Natasha Lamb, a director at Arjuna.[3]

workers share their wages with each other online and prefer companies that promote openness and equality.

IMPROVE FAMILY-FRIENDLY BENEFITS

The Family and Medical Leave Act of 1993, which lets employees take time off to care for themselves or a loved one, applies to employees in all public agencies and private companies with at least 50 employees. This leaves 39 percent of US workers without federally mandated leave. Only 12 percent of private companies have paid family leave, and that percentage has been decreasing since 2008.[4]

The lack of paid family and sick leave especially affects women because women are generally responsible for home care and childcare. In 2014, only 20 percent of the lowest-paid workers, primarily women, had paid sick leave, whereas 86 percent of the highest wage earners received this benefit. Without paid leave, many women experience financial

"THE ONE EMPLOYER WITH RELATIVELY FAIR PAY BETWEEN MEN AND WOMEN . . . IS THE FEDERAL GOVERNMENT. WHY? BECAUSE SALARY SCALES ARE PUBLISHED AND WIDELY KNOWN—SO WOMEN, WHO HISTORICALLY HAVE NOT NEGOTIATED FOR HIGHER SALARIES, OR ARE PUNISHED WHEN THEY DO—HAVE MORE INFORMATION ABOUT WHERE TO START."[5]

—BRIGID SCHULTE, AUTHOR OF *OVERWHELMED: WORK, LOVE AND PLAY WHEN NO ONE HAS TIME* hardship because they lose money staying home to care for themselves or other family members. Their other alternative is to go to work sick or neglect their families. Employers argue that if they are forced to provide paid leave, they will have to raise prices and offer employees fewer work hours and other benefits.

Childcare is another family-friendly benefit that is helpful to women. Government childcare subsidies exist for

MILLENNIALS DEMAND WORK/LIFE BALANCE

In late 2014 and early 2015, Ernst and Young, a financial services company, conducted a global survey of approximately 10,000 workers in eight countries. They discovered that 40 percent of US men and women in the millennial age range—born between 1982 and 2002—are so unhappy with the lack of government- and company-paid parental leave policies, they would be willing to move to another country with better policies.

the poor, but for most families, quality childcare can cost thousands of dollars each year. In 2014, childcare was the second-biggest expense for US families, after mortgage or rent payments. This means many women end up taking part-time work or poor-paying jobs with flexible hours to take care of their children. In most advanced countries, employers, unions, and governments share childcare costs with parents. The US Congress considered a universal childcare bill in the early 1970s, but President Richard M. Nixon vetoed it. A similar bill has not been considered since.

STRENGTHEN UNIONS

Studies have shown that people who belong to unions earn higher wages and have better working conditions and benefits than people not In unions. Women in unions earn approximately 30 percent more than women working in the same jobs who do not belong to unions. Women in unions have more paid leave, health insurance, and retirement benefits than women who are not union members.

The gender wage gap is smaller for women who belong to unions.

In 1983, 20 percent of US workers belonged to unions. In 2015, 11 percent were union members. People who favor unions say this decline is not only bad for women but for men as well. Unions tend to set higher industry standards that spread benefits to nonunion workers. Many employers contend that unions increase production costs too much and that they lose too much control over their workers.

RAISE THE FEDERAL MINIMUM WAGE AND TIPPED MINIMUM WAGE

The federal minimum wage has been $7.25 per hour since 2009. Raising the federal minimum wage to $12 an hour by 2020 would boost wages for more than 35 million working people, more than half of them women. Because so many women fill lower-paying jobs, raising the minimum wage would help reduce the wage gap. It would also help lift more than 2 million people out of poverty, many of them women.

Some economists argue that raising the minimum wage would cause employers to lay off workers and thereby increase unemployment. But research has shown that changes to the minimum wage have historically had little or no effect on unemployment. Instead, researchers have found that employers use other methods of dealing with increased labor costs, such as slightly raising prices, reducing training programs, or giving fewer raises and bonuses to upper-level workers. Some employers have found that increasing the minimum wages reduces turnover in their workforce, thus lowering the cost of training new employees. A few employers simply accept lower profits.

IN FAVOR OF RAISING THE MINIMUM WAGE

On January 14, 2014, more than 600 economists, including seven Nobel Prize winners, wrote a letter to President Obama and US congressional leaders. In the letter they said current research on the effect of raises to the minimum wage had little or no negative effect on the unemployment of minimum-wage workers. They went on to say that because these workers usually spend their increased earnings, there could even be a small stimulative effect on the economy.

The minimum wage for tipped workers in the United States is $2.13. Two-thirds of tipped-wages workers—such as restaurant servers—are women. Including tips, women earn $10.07 per hour, on average, whereas their male counterparts average $10.63 per hour.[6] Eliminating the tipped minimum wage and replacing it with at least the current

94

federal minimum wage would raise the wages of millions of service workers. Restaurants and other service-industry companies argue that eliminating the tipped minimum wage would increase expenses and increase unwanted government interference in the marketplace.

STRENGTHEN AND ENFORCE LABOR LAWS

Research suggests that gender discrimination plays a role in hiring and pay, and some economists believe enforcing existing equal-pay laws could help reduce discrimination. Enforcement would include prosecuting employers who violate wage discrimination laws, and requiring employers to demonstrate that hiring, pay, and promotions are not based on gender. Each year, employers steal $50 billion from employees by not paying them the wages they are owed.[7] Some employers also fail to pay the minimum wage, overtime pay, Social Security taxes, or state and federal taxes.

Women are more likely to have their wages stolen, partly because they work in jobs with proven wage theft problems, such as restaurant servers. One way to combat wage theft is for federal and state governments to strongly enforce existing laws, with heavy penalties for perpetrators. Some economists also recommend strong unions as a solution to help protect members' legal rights.

TIE WAGES TO PRODUCTIVITY

For four decades, US workers have been working harder but their wages have generally stayed the same. For example, a product or task that used to require five people now takes only four people. This increased productivity, with no rise in wages, means each product or service costs less to produce, so it makes more money when it is sold. The people who run large corporations have done well, whereas lower- and middle-class workers have struggled.

At first, productivity/wage inequity was worse for men than for women. But because

NO GENDER WAGE GAP AT AMAZON?

In 2015, the online retailer Amazon released a report on its gender wage gap. The report revealed that women earned 99.9 cents for every dollar men earned doing the same job. Minorities made 100.1 cents for every dollar made by white workers in the same job. In Amazon's global workforce, approximately 39 percent were women, and women made up 24 percent of managers.[8] Amazon did not explain its lack of a wage gap. Critics of the report argued that because Amazon employed far fewer women than men, especially in upper management, the overall wage gap must actually be much higher.

women have continued to enter the workforce and tend to be employed in lower-paying jobs, the productivity/wage gap means women's wages have also stagnated. One proposed solution to the wage gap is for the federal government to enact labor regulations that tie increased wages to increased productivity for those in low- and moderate-wage jobs. Because women disproportionately fill low-wage jobs, they would be the biggest beneficiaries of increased wages, thereby helping to shrink the gender wage gap.

GENDER PAY GAP AMONG CHILDREN

It appears that a gender wage gap exists even for children. A national survey conducted in Australia in 2013 revealed that boys earned $48 per week in allowance, whereas girls earned $45 per week doing more work. Girls spent 2.7 hours on average doing chores, such as dishes and cleaning, whereas boys spent 2.1 hours on chores, such as mowing the lawn and taking out trash. As one journalist noted, "Paying girls less than boys sends a powerful message that girls and women's work just isn't as valuable as boy's."[9]

ENCOURAGE WOMEN TO ENTER HIGHER-PAYING PROFESSIONS

According to many experts, the job gap, in which women tend to segregate into lower-paying jobs whereas men segregate into higher-paying jobs, is one of the biggest reasons for the current 78-cent overall wage gap. Women do make choices that affect their earnings, such as pursuing college degrees in lower-paying fields. To combat this trend, schoolteachers and counselors can encourage girls who are interested in science, technology, engineering, and math to enter these careers. Teachers and counselors can also make girls aware of the differences in pay between different industries and professions.

The gender wage gap will continue to narrow. But it will take the cooperation of businesses, governments, and women themselves—along with changes in societal expectations about what is men's work and women's work—to make it finally close for good.

Women all around the world are fighting to close the gender wage gap for future generations.

ESSENTIAL
FACTS

MAJOR EVENTS

- The first national minimum wage law in the United States—the Fair Labor Standards Act (FLSA)—is passed in 1938. The law requires a minimum wage of 25 cents per hour and a maximum workweek of 44 hours.

- The Equal Pay Act is passed in 1963. The act prohibits sex-based wage discrimination between men and women in the same job in the same company.

- The Lilly Ledbetter Fair Pay Act is passed in 2009. The law protects against gender wage discrimination.

KEY PLAYERS

- Barak Obama signs the Lilly Ledbetter Fair Pay Act into law and issues executive orders aimed at promoting gender wage equality.

- Lilly Ledbetter, a manager for Goodyear Tire & Rubber Company, sues for discrimination when she discovers she is not being paid the same as her male peers. Though she loses her case in the US Supreme Court, she becomes the namesake of the law that corrects the technicality that prevented her from winning.

IMPACT ON SOCIETY

Besides the inherent unfairness of women being paid less than men for doing the same jobs, experts associate real social and economic costs with the gender wage gap. Studies have shown that companies with more women in charge make more money. Women who are disproportionately concentrated in low-paying jobs struggle with poverty, and depression, and they often have to make hard choices between working and taking care of their families. Women who earn less than men are more likely to be on government assistance programs. Many women with college degrees are unable to put their educations to full use because they must choose temporary or part-time jobs to take care of their families. The economic and personal impacts of the gender wage gap affect women, their families, and the societies they live in.

QUOTE

"It is fitting that with the very first bill I sign—the Lilly Ledbetter Fair Pay Act—we are upholding one of this nation's first principles: that we are all created equal and each deserve a chance to pursue our own version of happiness."

—*President Barack Obama, January 29, 2009*

GLOSSARY

AMENDMENT
A formal addition or change to a document.

DISCRIMINATION
Unfair treatment of other people, usually because of race, age, or gender.

DISSENT
To express a different opinion from others.

FILIBUSTER
An action, such as a prolonged speech, that obstructs progress in a legislature.

GRIEVANCE
A real or imagined cause for complaint or protest, especially unfair treatment.

HACKER
A person who uses computers to gain unauthorized access to another computer in order to view, copy, or destroy data.

NEGOTIATE

To attempt to reach an agreement or compromise through discussion.

PATRIARCHAL

Characteristic of a system of society or government controlled by men.

SEGREGATE

To separate groups of people based on race, gender, ethnicity, or other factors.

SOCIOLOGIST

A person who studies the development, structure, and functioning of human society.

STEREOTYPE

A widely held but oversimplified idea about a particular type of person or thing.

SWEATSHOP

A type of factory where manual laborers are employed for low pay and are forced to work long hours under poor conditions.

ADDITIONAL
RESOURCES

SELECTED BIBLIOGRAPHY

Alter, Charlotte. "Here's the History of the Battle for Equal Pay for American Women." *Time*. Time, 14 Apr. 2015. Web. 28 June 2016.

Cho, Rosa, and Abagail Kramer. "Everything You Need to Know about the Equal Pay Act." *Re:Gender*. Re:Gender, 2016. Web. 28 June 2016.

Davis, Alyssa, and Elise Gould. "Closing the Pay Gap and Beyond." *Economic Policy Institute*. Economic Policy Institute, 18 Nov. 2015. Web. 28 June 2016.

Schulte, Brigid. "The Wage Gap: A Primer." *Washington Post*. Washington Post, 2 Oct. 2014. Web. 28 June 2016.

FURTHER READINGS

Merino, Nöel, ed. *The Wage Gap*. Detroit: Greenhaven, 2014. Print.

Vapnek, Lara. *Breadwinners: Working Women and Economic Independence, 1865–1920*. Urbana: U of Illinois P, 2009. Print.

WEBSITES

To learn more about Special Reports, visit **booklinks.abdopublishing.com**. These links are routinely monitored and updated to provide the most current information available.

FOR MORE INFORMATION

For more information on this subject, contact or visit the following organizations:

The US Capitol
East Capitol Street NE and 1st Street NE
Washington, DC 20002
202-226-8000
http://www.visitthecapitol.gov
The US Capitol is an architecturally significant building where members of the Senate and House of Representatives discuss, debate, and pass federal legislation. Tours are available.

US Equal Employment Opportunity Commission (EEOC)
131 M Street NE
Washington, DC 20507
202-663-4900
http://www.eeoc.gov/index.cfm
The EEOC is responsible for enforcing federal wage discrimination laws.

SOURCE NOTES

CHAPTER 1. SHEDDING LIGHT ON THE WAGE GAP

1. Mike Fleming Jr. "Bart & Fleming: Why Jennifer Lawrence's Ballsy 'American Hustle' Payday Rant Isn't Anatomically Correct." *Deadline Hollywood*. Penske Business, 18 Oct. 2015. Web. 5 July 2016.

2. Ibid.

3. Aly Weisman. "Leaked: Jennifer Lawrence Got American Hustled in Sony Deal." *Business Insider*. Business Insider, 14 Dec. 2014. Web. 5 July 2016.

4. Natalie Robehmed. "The World's Highest-Paid Actresses 2015: Jennifer Lawrence Leads with $52 Million." *Forbes*. Forbes, 20 Aug. 2015. Web. 5 July 2016.

5. Jennifer Lawrence. "Why Do I Make Less Than My Male Co-Stars?" *Lenny*. Lenny, 13 Oct. 2015. Web. 5 July 2016.

6. Ibid.

7. Sara Ashley O'Brien. "78 Cents on the Dollar: The Facts about the Gender Wage Gap." *CNN Money*. Cable News Network, 14 Apr. 2015. Web. 5 July 2016.

8. Aly Weisman. "Leaked: Jennifer Lawrence Got American Hustled in Sony Deal." *Business Insider*. Business Insider, 14 Dec. 2014. Web. 5 July 2016.

9. Carrie Lukas. "The Equal Pay Myth." *Policy Focus*. Independent Women's Forum, Apr. 2012. Web. 5 July 2016.

10. Catherine Hill. "The Simple Truth about the Gender Pay Gap (Spring 2016)." *AAUW*. AAUW, n.d. Web. 5 July 2016.

11. Ambereen Choudhury. "Women Earn Wages Equivalent to 2006 Male Level, WEF Reports Says." *Bloomberg*. Bloomberg, 18 Nov. 2015. Web. 5 July 2016.

CHAPTER 2. BATTLING FOR EQUAL PAY

1. Alexandra Lutz. "Labor Conditions during the Second Industrial Revolution." *Study.com*. Study.com, n.d. Web. 5 July 2016.

2. Jonathan Grossman. "Fair Labor Standards Act of 1938: Maximum Struggle for Minimum Wage." *United States Department of Labor*. US Department of Labor, n.d. Web. 5 July 2016.

3. Charlotte Alter. "Here's the History of the Battle for Equal Pay for American Women." *Time*. Time, 14 Apr. 2015. Web. 28 June 2016.

4. "Fair Labor Standards Act." *United States History*. United States History, n.d. Web. 18 July 2016.

5. Allan Carlson. *The Family in America: Searching for Social Harmony in the Industrial Age*. New Brunswick, NJ: Transaction, 2009. *Google Book Search*. Web. 5 July 2016.

6. Rani Molla. "Women's Pay Compared to Men's from 1960 to 2013." *Wall Street Journal.* Wall Street Journal, 23 Sep. 2014. Web. 5 July 2016.

7. Rosa Cho and Abagail Kramer. "Everything You Need to Know about the Equal Pay Act." *Re:Gender.* Re:Gender, 2016. Web. 5 July 2016.

8. Richard E. Schumann. "Compensation from World War II through the Great Society." *US Bureau of Labor Statistics.* US Bureau of Labor Statistics, 30 Jan. 2003. Web. 5 July 2016.

CHAPTER 3. FACTORS AFFECTING THE WAGE GAP

1. Rosa Cho and Abagail Kramer. "Everything You Need to Know about the Equal Pay Act." *Re:Gender.* Re:Gender, 2016. Web. 5 July 2016.

2. Sarah Jane Glynn. "Explaining the Gender Wage Gap." *Center for American Progress.* Center for American Progress, 19 May 2014. Web. 5 July 2016.

3. Sarah Bryan Miller. "In Orchestras, a Sea Change in Gender Proportions." *St. Louis Post-Dispatch.* St. Louis Post-Dispatch, 30 Mar. 2014 Web. 5 July 2016.

4. Rani Molla. "Women's Pay Compared to Men's from 1960 to 2013." *Wall Street Journal.* Wall Street Journal, 23 Sep. 2014. Web. 5 July 2016.

5. Sarah Jane Glynn. "Explaining the Gender Wage Gap." *Center for American Progress.* Center for American Progress, 19 May 2014. Web. 5 July 2016.

6. "Family Structure and Children's Living Arrangements." *ChildStats.gov.* ChildStats.gov, n.d. Web. 5 July 2016.

7. Libby Nelson. "For the First Time Ever, More American Women Than Men Are College Graduates." *Vox.* Vox Media, 13 Oct. 2015. Web. 5 July 2016.

8. Dr. Andrew Chamberlain. "New Research: Demystifying the Gender Pay Gap." *Huffington Post.* HuffPost, 25 Mar. 2016. Web. 5 July 2016.

CHAPTER 4. ENTERTAINMENT AND SPORTS

1. Natalie Robehmed. "The World's Highest-Paid Actresses 2015: Jennifer Lawrence Leads with $52 Million." *Forbes.* Forbes, 20 Aug. 2015. Web. 5 July 2016.

2. Lucy Clarke-Billings. "Meryl Streep: I Still Experience Sexism and Get Paid Less than Men." *Telegraph.* Telegraph Media Group, 10 Oct. 2015. Web. 5 July 2016.

3. Martha M. Lauzen. "Independent Women: Behind-the-Scenes Employment on Festival Films in 2013–14." *Center for the Study of Women in Television & Film.* Dr. Martha Lauzen, 2016. Web. 5 July 2016.

4. Natalie Robehmed. "The World's Highest-Paid Actresses 2015: Jennifer Lawrence Leads with $52 Million." *Forbes.* Forbes, 20 Aug. 2015. Web. 5 July 2016.

5. Natalie Robehmed. "The World's Highest-Paid Actors 2015: Robert Downey Jr. Leads with $80 Million Haul." *Forbes.* Forbes, 4 Aug. 2015. Web. 5 July 2016.

6. Jake Coyle. "Correction: Entertainment Equality Study Story." *AP Big Story.* Associated Press, 18 Mar. 2016. Web. 5 July 2016.

7. Zack O'Malley Greenburg. "The World's Highest-Paid Musicians of 2015." *Forbes.* Forbes, 8 Dec. 2015. Web. 5 July 2016.

8. Zack O'Malley Greenburg. "The Celebrity 100: Aftermath & Analysis 2015." *Forbes.* Forbes, 7 July 2015. Web. 5 July 2016.

9. Jenny Stevens and Ami Sedghi. "Glastonbury, Reading or Creamfields: Which 2015 Festival Has the Fewest Female Artists?" *Guardian.* Guardian News, 23 June 2015. Web. 5 July 2016.

10. Hannah Thacker. "Women in the Music Industry." *Humanhuman.* HumanHuman, 2016. Web. 5 July 2016.

11. "Novak Djokovic: Men's Tennis Should Fight for More Prize Money Than Women." *Guardian.* Guardian News, 21 Mar. 2016. Web. 5 July 2016.

12. Miguel Morales. "Tennis' Gender Pay Gap Problem Looms on the Sidelines." *Forbes.* Forbes, 21 Feb 2014. Web. 5 July 2016.

SOURCE NOTES
CONTINUED

13. "Pay Inequity in Athletics." *Women's Sports Foundation.* Women's Sports Foundation, 2011. Web. 5 July 2016.

14. "US Soccer Asks EEOC to Dismiss Complaint of Wage Discrimination." *ESPNW.* ESPN, 31 May 2016. Web. 5 July 2016.

CHAPTER 5. OTHER INDUSTRIES

1. Valentina Zarya. "1 in 5 HR Managers Admit That Women at Their Companies Get Paid Less Than Men." *Fortune.* Fortune, 26 Feb. 2016. Web. 5 July 2016.

2. "Household Data Annual Averages." *Bureau of Labor Statistics.* Bureau of Labor Statistics, 2015. Web. 5 July 2016.

3. Eric Yoder. "Government Workforce Is Closing the Gender Pay Gap, but Reforms Still Needed, Reports Says." *Washington Post.* Washington Post, 13 Apr. 2014. Web. 5 July 2016.

4. Kristen Bellstrom. "Why 2015 Was a Terrible Year to Be a Female Fortune 500 CEO." *Fortune.* Fortune, 23 Dec. 2015. Web. 5 July 2016.

5. Aaron Taube. "'Lean In' Isn't Enough: Women's Progress in Leadership Has Stalled." *Business Insider.* Business Insider, 23 Sep. 2014. Web. 5 July 2016.

6. Rose Pastore. "How the 10 Highest-Paid Women CEOs Compare to Their Male Counterparts." *Fast Company.* Fast Company, 29 May 2015. Web. 5 July 2016.

7. Owen Davis. "Why Women Executives Get Paid Less Than Male Counterparts—New Fed Study Explains." *International Business Times.* IBT Media, 25 Mar. 2015. Web. 5 July 2016.

8. Kelley Holland. "Careers with the Biggest Gender Pay Gap." *USA Today.* USA Today, 26 Mar. 2016. Web. 5 July 2016.

9. Margaret Magnarelli. "The 25 Careers with the Smallest Wage Gaps for Women." *Money.* Time, 14 Apr. 2015. Web. 5 July 2016.

10. Drake Baer and Andy Kiersz. "Here Are the Only 9 Jobs in America Where Women Outearn Men." *Business Insider.* Business Insider, 24 Mar. 2015. Web. 6 July 2016.

11. Kellie Lunney. "Government Makes Another Move to Eliminate Gender Pay Gap." *Government Executive.* National Journal Group, 5 Aug. 2015. Web. 5 July 2016.

CHAPTER 6. A GLOBAL PROBLEM

1. Elaine Moore. "Gender Pay Gap Shows Little Sign of Closing." *Financial Times.* Financial Times, 26 Feb. 2014. Web. 5 July 2016.

2. "Global Gender Gap Report 2015." *World Economic Forum.* World Economic Forum, 2016. Web. 5 July 2016.

3. Naomi Grimley. "Gender Pay Gap 'May Take 118 Years to Close'—World Economic Forum." *BBC.* BBC News, 19 Nov. 2015. Web. 5 July 2016.

4. "National Living Wage Comes into Force." *BBC News.* BBC, 1 Apr. 2016. Web. 5 July 2016.

5. "Global Gender Gap Report 2015." *World Economic Forum.* World Economic Forum, 2016. Web. 5 July 2016.

6. Joanne Lipman. "Let's Expose the Gender Pay Gap." *New York Times.* New York Times, 13 Aug. 2015. Web. 5 July 2016.

7. Danielle Paquette. "Rwanda Is Beating the United States in Gender Equality." *Washington Post.* Washington Post, 20 Nov. 2015. Web. 5 July 2016.

8. Katrin Park. "S. Korea Reflects Lag in Gender Equality: Column." *USA Today.* USA Today, 14 Mar. 2015. Web. 5 July 2016.

9. Choe Sang-Hun. "Korean Women Flock to Government." *New York Times.* New York Times, 1 Mar. 2010. Web. 5 July 2016.

CHAPTER 7. RECENT WAGE GAP LEGISLATION

1. Rosa Cho and Abagail Kramer. "Everything You Need to Know about the Equal Pay Act." *Re:Gender.* Re:Gender, 2016. Web. 5 July 2016.

2. "Summaries for the Paycheck Fairness Act." *Govtrack.us.* GovTrack, 14 Feb. 2016. Web. 5 July 2016.

3. Ibid.

4. Sheryl Gay Stolberg. "Obama Signs Equal-Pay Legislation." *New York Times.* New York Times, 29 Jan. 2009. Web. 5 July 2016.

5. Rosa Cho and Abagail Kramer. "Everything You Need to Know about the Equal Pay Act." *Re:Gender.* Re:Gender, 2016. Web. 5 July 2016.

6. "Obama's National Equal Pay Enforcement Task Force and Equal Pay Initiative: Equal Chance for a Pay Audit for You?" *Workplace Insights.* Capital Associated Industries, 7 June 2010. Web. 5 July 2016.

7. Danielle Paquette and Drew Harwell. "Obama Targets Gender Pay Gap with Plan to Collect Companies' Salary Data." *Washington Post.* Washington Post, 29 Jan. 2016. Web. 5 July 2016.

8. Ibid.

CHAPTER 8. HOW TO SHRINK THE WAGE GAP

1. Bill Quigley. "Top Ten Arguments for Raising the Minimum Wage." *Huffington Post.* Huffington Post, 16 May 2015. Web. 5 July 2016.

2. Jena McGregor. "The Worst Question You Could Ask Women in a Job Interview." *Washington Post.* Washington Post, 14 Apr. 2015. Web. 5 July 2016.

3. Jena McGregor. "Amazon, Amid Pressure from an Investor, Reports Virtually No Gender Pay Gap." *Washington Post.* Washington Post, 24 Mar. 2016. Web. 5 July 2016

4. Brigid Schulte. "Millennials Want a Work-Life Balance. Their Bosses Just Don't Get Why." *Washington Post.* Washington Post, 5 May 2015. Web. 5 July 2016.

5. Brigid Schulte. "The Wage Gap: A Primer." *Washington Post.* Washington Post, 2 Oct. 2014. Web. 5 July 2016.

6. Alyssa Davis and Elise Gould. "Closing the Pay Gap and Beyond." *Economic Policy Institute.* Economic Policy Institute, 18 Nov. 2015. Web. 5 July 2016.

7. Ibid.

8. Angel Gonzalez. "Amazon Says There's No Gender or Ethnic Wage Gaps in Its Ranks." *Seattle Times.* Seattle Times, 12 Apr. 2016. Web. 5 July 2016.

9. Kasey Edwards. "The Gender Pay Gap Exists among Children." *Daily Life.* Fairfax Media, 23 July 2013. Web. 5 July 2016.

INDEX

ABOUT THE
AUTHORS

Melissa Higgins writes fiction and nonfiction for children and young adults. Two of her novels for struggling readers, *Bi-Normal* and *I'm Just Me*, won silver medals in the Independent Publisher (IPPY) Book Awards. Higgins' nearly 60 nonfiction titles range from character development and psychology to history and biographies. When not writing, Higgins enjoys hiking and taking photographs around her home in the Arizona desert.

Michael Regan, MEd, worked for 30 years as a middle-school and college counselor and advisor before turning his attention to research and writing. He is especially interested in topics related to technology and current events. He lives in the southwestern United States.